The Servant Songs of Isaiah 40–55

Interpreting Old Testament Prophecy

Philip Jenson

Lecturer in Old Testament, Ridley Hall

GROVE BOOKS LIMITED

RIDLEY HALL RD CAMBRIDGE CB3 9HU

Contents

First Impression June 2020
ISSN 1365-490X
ISBN 978 1 78827 125 7

The Long Way Round

1

In the entire Old Testament is there a clearer or more persuasive prophecy about Jesus Christ than Isaiah 53? A servant of God, growing up before him like a young plant, nothing impressive about his appearance, leading a life without violence or deceit, a man of suffering, rejected by others, despised, silent before his accusers, taken away by a perversion of justice, wounded for our transgressions, bearing our iniquities, giving his life as a sacrifice for sin, bearing the punishment that made us whole, making many righteous, cut off from the land of the living, given a tomb with the rich, but who sees light, is exalted and made very high, prolongs his days, silences kings and startles nations.

We are even more convinced if we link this impressive prediction to three other texts in Isaiah 40–55, each of which refers to a special servant of the Lord. Scholars have called these the Servant Songs (SS).

	Text	**Brief summary of servant's character and role**
SS1	Isa 42.1–7 (or 1–4)	God's chosen, filled with his spirit, to establish justice in the earth, be a light to the nations
SS2	Isa 49.1–7 (or 1–9)	Laboured in vain, restorer of Israel, a light to the nations, acknowledged by kings
SS3	Isa 50.4–11 (or 4–9)	Tongue of a teacher, does not hide his face from insults, the Lord will help and vindicate him
SS4	Isa 52.13–53.12 ('Isaiah 53' for brevity)	Suffers despite being innocent, wounded for our transgressions, exalted and lifted up

Who else could this suffering servant be except Jesus? This appears to be true beyond doubt whenever we hear these texts read alongside the gospel in church. This is especially the case on Good Friday when Isaiah 53 is read alongside the passion narrative. It is confirmed in our ears whenever we hear Handel's musical masterpiece, *The Messiah*. He sets no fewer than five movements to verses from Isaiah 53, more than any other Scripture. The same text has profoundly influenced the visual portrayal of the crucifixion in the Western tradition. Earlier the cross was generally seen to be a sign of the majesty and victory of Christ. The face of Christ is compassionate and serene. But from medieval times onwards meditation on Isaiah 53 influenced the extreme portrayals of the suffering and agony of Christ.[1]

And yet, and yet! Many remain unpersuaded. Most evident are a host of Jewish readers of the text, past and present. Thus the great medieval Jewish exegete Rashi sees the suffering of the Jewish people in Isaiah 53. He proposes that the prophet 'mentions all Israel as one man,' as he does elsewhere (Isa 44.1–2).[2] It is sobering to remember that many Jews read the original Hebrew text and know it far better than Christians, yet the great majority do not find Jesus in it. They point out that Christians only pick out those features of the text that they can apply to Jesus, and ignore others that do not.

The study of the Servant Songs is a lesson in multiple reading

Many honoured Jesus highly during his ministry, so that he was by no means despised. He was notorious for speaking boldly, and at length. Even during his trial, his silence was temporary and exceptional (Matt 26.63; Mark 14.61-62). He was the only person in his tomb, so was not buried with the rich and the wicked. Nor did he have any offspring in the normal sense of the word. Of course, a Christian might object that this is too literalistic a reading, but who decides how a word or phrase is to be interpreted? Every reader interprets the Bible within the framework of a larger set of assumptions and beliefs. These guide what aspects of the text are noticed, and which are left in the background without comment. The story of the study of the Servant Songs is a lesson in multiple readings, depending on who the reader is and their context and interests. The openness, metaphorical richness, and poetic allusiveness of the Servant Songs make this inevitable and unavoidable.

The Questions of Historical Criticism

Historical criticism has its own doubts and questions that also need to be heard. If the Bible is a human production that has a history, then it should make sense in its historical context, even though such an approach to interpreting need not be the only one. Until the nineteenth century it was generally assumed that the whole of the book was written by Isaiah, the eighth-century prophet of Jerusalem. But from a historical point of view, this is likely to be an over-simplification. The distinctive language and historical setting of Isaiah 40–55 is very different from most of Isaiah 1–39.

Instead, there are numerous indications of an exilic setting (the sixth century BC), not least the specific references to the Persian king Cyrus. The main purpose of this section of Isaiah is to encourage the exiles to return to Jerusalem, which would be strange if it was dated two centuries earlier. Nor does it make historical sense if it predicts events in detail that will happen hundreds of years in the future. That only happens in modern fanciful fiction and TV drama! For most modern scholars the Servant Songs should make sense in their own context, although this does not exclude other ways of reading

Isaiah.[3] This does not undermine in any way the inspired and authoritative nature of these texts, nor the importance of reading the Book of Isaiah as a unity. For the exilic author of Isaiah 40–55 (whom we can call Second Isaiah) takes up many of the themes and hopes of the prophet Isaiah.[4] Nevertheless, the historical critical approach has made it difficult to hold the view that the Servant Songs referred originally to Jesus. We need to look for an approach to these texts that does justice both to their historical nature and to how they speak of Jesus Christ.

The idea that there are good ways of reading Isaiah 53 without reference to Jesus can disturb faithful Christians when they come across it. They assume what I call the Jesus short-cut. For us, in the light of the New Testament, all kinds of Old Testament texts seem to point to Christ, and invite us to affirm with wonder and joy, 'This is that which was spoken by the prophet' (Acts 2.16, KJV).[5] This, I believe, is not incorrect. But I do not think that it will satisfy anyone who recognizes that the Bible should make sense in its historical context. The questions that historical criticism asks deserve careful consideration. The Jesus short-cut is like copying down just the answer to an exam question, without setting out all the steps that led to it. It is skipping to the end of a detective story to find the identity of the murderer, without appreciating the motives and moves of the key players.

Reading Isaiah 53 without reference to Jesus can disturb faithful Christians

The Old Testament takes us through a rich, complex and fascinating story, which includes a great deal of revolutionary development. At each stage we discover fresh insights into how God is at work amongst his people and in the world. In the Old Testament, as in our lives, God's way of working is often slow, indirect and surprising. Taking the long way round, rather than the easy short-cut, demands patience and careful attention to the text of Scripture. But I hope that when we eventually reach our destination, we shall perceive with a greater wonder and a deeper thankfulness how God speaks to us through the Scriptures and in his Son Jesus Christ.

2 Metaphors of Prophetic Prediction

How do the prophets speak about the future? The Jesus short-cut may have some flaws, but it will remain the only option unless there are alternative accounts of the process. In this chapter I would like to explore four models or metaphors. The first of these underlies the Jesus short-cut. The other three offer more flexible and, I believe, more realistic approaches to prophecy.

The Cannonball Metaphor

The Jesus short-cut is effectively working with a model of causation that is rigid and unalterable. We can picture it as the prophet firing a cannonball (the prophecy) towards a distant target (the future event). There is not much that can affect the trajectory of a cannonball. It either hits where it is aimed, or it does not. In this model the fulfilment of prophecy is a simple yes/no judgment. Like a horoscope or a weather forecast, it is basically either right or wrong. It is a model that does work well with short-term prophecies, such as when Elijah predicts a drought (1 Kgs 17.1) or Micaiah prophecies the defeat of Israel and Judah (Isa 22.17). The accuracy of these short-term predictions is the criterion used to discern a true or false prophet in Deut 18.22.

However, it is rather different with longer-term prophecies, especially in the poetry of the prophets. These tend to be more open and ambiguous. It is hard to tell what is symbol or hyperbole. Extending the cannonball metaphor to these is problematic. A sceptic would point to the problem of prophecies that were not fulfilled by Jesus. For example, the coming king was meant to return Jews to their homeland (Isa 43.5-6), rebuild the temple (Ezek 37.26–28) and bring about a messianic age of peace (Isa 2.4). Jesus brought about none of these.

It is possible to take them into account, but such an adjustment of the cannonball metaphor makes it less and less helpful. One alternative is the double mountain peak model. Some prophecies are fulfilled in Christ's first coming (the first mountain peak), but others at his second coming (the second and final peak). From a Christian perspective Old Testament prophets did not distinguish these, just as a hiker might see what appears to be the top of a hill, only to find out that a further peak hides beyond it.

The prophets glimpse what needs to happen, but are not aware of the precise how and when. But this does still not do justice to the profound changes that the prophecy has undergone through time. For example, the New Testament understanding of the temple of God as referring to the people and not the building is not one that the Old Testament envisages. Even Christians can be somewhat embarrassed by the strained nature of some New Testament citations of Old Testament texts, which appear to have been taken out of context. For example, from a historical point of view it is very unlikely that Isa 7.14 refers to a virgin birth.[6] How do we evaluate Matthew's radical interpretation of this verse as a literal virgin birth (Matt 1.22–23)? Something more complicated is at work here than a simple one or two stage fulfilment.

The simplicity and confidence of the cannonball model is attractive, especially in an age that prizes mathematical precision and scientific accuracy. Such an approach is behind the popular charts listing Old Testament prophecies with their New Testament fulfilment. The model invites impressive mathematical calculations. If 50 or 100 prophecies are fulfilled by Jesus, and each of them has a one in two chance of happening, then the odds on all of them happening are astronomical.

The only conclusion that can be drawn is that Jesus is the miraculous fulfilment of divinely inspired prophecy. But this does not do justice to the openness of prophecy, or to non-fulfilments. Nor does it take account of the way in which Jesus intentionally patterned his life according to prophecy. It can hardly count as an independent fulfilment when Jesus deliberately chose to ride a donkey into Jerusalem (Zech 9.9; Matt 21.1–5).

The Bird Metaphor

The cannonball model neglects the complex story behind the words that we read in our Bible today. Words and prophecies do not have a fixed, unchanging meaning. Prophecies are winged words. They are birds, released into the wild by their creators, whose precise flight cannot be controlled. From early on readers understood the prophetic oracles to have an ongoing relevance beyond their first audience. Editors collected and revised them for future generations. Translators further updated and adapted them to other languages and cultures.

Prophecies are birds whose precise flight cannot be controlled

The changing contexts in which they were transmitted profoundly influenced these prophecies. We may compare how birds are influenced by the winds and the storms that they encounter on their migrations. Frequently they cannot go directly as the crow flies, but must take the long way round. Yet eventually they reach their destination, or something that fulfils the same purpose. Sometimes birds will come across a location that fulfils all that they wished for as a base for feeding and breeding. Understanding a prophecy requires us to trace its journey, including detours, digressions and unexpected fulfilments. Only when we have done this can we discern what is central to the message, and what is contingent upon specific conditions. The meaning of the text changes and develops as it is revised, and again when it is reread in the light of other Scriptures.

One example of this is the prediction of the return of the people of Israel to the land. Some forms of Zionism see these as having been proved true by the return of Jews to the land of Israel. But the New Testament transforms these prophecies into a larger hope of a new creation. The prophetic word has in its flight discovered a destination that was richer and broader than its author could ever have imagined. So it is for the Servant Songs. Even if we were able to discover their original meaning, this does not define what they might come to mean in the larger context of the Book of Isaiah, or the Old Testament, or the coming of Christ.

The Improvisation Metaphor

It is striking that the New Testament authors appear to read the Old Testament with considerable freedom and creativity. Another helpful metaphor is that of jazz improvisation. A jazz musician has the freedom to improvise on a theme. Rather than reproducing exactly the notes of a score, the approach is selective, indirect and innovative, usually incorporating elements that are not in the original. In the same way later biblical writers worked freely with inherited texts in what is called inner-biblical interpretation. They build on what has been received, but adapt it to their own context and concerns. Sometimes these interpretations are very different, but there is some degree of continuity.

They build on what has been received, but adapt it to their own context and concerns

Similarly the solos by the members of a jazz group are often forcefully individual, but the overall performance is unified by the common theme and the underlying harmonic structure. Our enjoyment comes from recognizing what is familiar, combined with an appreciation of the transformations of the theme. As we grow in our knowledge of jazz we become aware how the interpretation reflects the style, interests and cultural setting of the musicians.

Hugh Williamson has suggested that something similar is happening in the Book of Isaiah.[7] The different stages of the book represent variations on a theme. The theme is human and divine kingship, and the three main sections of the book provide distinct portrayals of their relationship in a way that demonstrates both radical difference and an underlying common purpose. In Isaiah 1–39 the weaknesses of human kingship are probed, combined with texts setting out a vision for the ideal king. These include the well-known Christmas readings (Isa 7.1–16; 9.1–7; 11.1-9). In Isaiah 40–55 the language of human kingship disappears and instead it proclaims the kingship of the Lord, the God of Israel. The traditional role of the king in Israel was to mediate between God and his people, for better or for worse. In Isaiah 1–39 there is a dramatic contrast between Ahaz (Isa 7.10–13) and Hezekiah (Isaiah 36–39). But now the people are called to take on the role of the Davidic king (Isa 55.3). They are to witness to the Lord's rule over the cosmos and history.

Finally in Isaiah 56–66 the universal implications of God's cosmic kingship become evident. Membership of God's people and the call to serve the Lord are opened up to eunuchs and foreigners (Isa 56.1–8). The sovereign purposes of God will result in the salvation of Zion, alongside the creation of a new heavens and a new earth (Isa 65.17). In his life and death Jesus gives us a virtuoso performance of the Servant Songs that transforms them, while retaining the underlying melody and harmony.

The Recycling Metaphor

Recycling is a particularly attractive metaphor as we become ever more aware of the consequences of our throwaway culture. Like metal or high-quality plastic, the words of the Lord have a true and permanent quality that transcends any particular situation. They can be reapplied to any number of similar situations. This is what typically happens in preaching, when words in a book from long ago and far away are applied to the lives of a particular congregation. This can be a very close parallel, but sometimes there is a creative application that the original authors could never have imagined. As in recycling, the adaptation can be relatively small (as when glass milk bottles are reused after washing) or pronounced (as when plastic is turned into pellets that can be incorporated into quite different products).

As in recycling, the adaptation can be relatively small or pronounced

This is what we find in the Bible as well. A classic example is the voice crying out, 'Prepare the way of the Lord' (Isa 40.3). The evangelists recycle this to indicate the significance of the ministry of John the Baptist (Matt 3.3; Mark 1.3; Luke 3.4). The call to return from Babylon becomes a call to turn away in repentance from sin. The servant figure is particularly good material for recycling because of its ambiguity. And while the application to Jesus is particularly apt, we shall see that this does not exclude further recycling.

Evaluating the Metaphors

All these metaphors have strengths, as well as aspects that do not fit the reality to which they point and so should not be activated. The cannonball metaphor is the simplest, but also the most restricted in scope in being best fitted to short-term prophecies. It does not do justice to the openness and complexity either of the longer reach of prophecy, or how later interpreters (including Jesus) read it. The other three models pay more attention to how later readers understood the prophecy in different ways at different times. Biblical prophecy is not a collection of timeless predictions. They form part of an ongoing and developing conversation between God and his people. They undertake a long and arduous journey towards their fulfilment in Christ. Doing justice to this story requires the long way round.

The Servant Songs

3

Let us return to the Servant Songs, although first we should recognize that not all scholars regard them as a well-defined group of texts. Separating them out for individual treatment is a recent move in biblical scholarship. Only in 1892 did the great German scholar Bernard Duhm isolate these four texts and group them together.[8] He himself thought that they were written by a different author, and a later editor inserted them into the text. However, there is so much similarity between the Songs and the rest of Isaiah 40–55 that almost all scholars consider them to have the same author. And if they have the same author, should we be separating them from the rest of Isaiah 40–55 and treating them independently? A significant proportion of scholars think that we should declare 'Farewell to the Servant Songs,' and acknowledge that these texts are one with the rest of Second Isaiah.[9] They do not have a different poetic genre or style from the rest of Second Isaiah, so even calling them songs is misleading.

'Servant' appears to refer to two different entities who are related but not identical

Yet many interpreters continue to find in them a certain distinctiveness. Above all, 'servant' appears to refer to two rather different entities who are inextricably related but not identical. The first is Israel as a whole, and the primary object of God's grace and calling. They are all those who call Abraham their ancestral father and Sarah their ancestral mother (Isa 51.2). This servant is often found in verses where Israel and Jacob are named in parallel lines (Isa 41.8; 44.1). But there are also indications of a second kind of servant, who is distinct from Israel as a whole and has a special role towards the nation. This is the servant who comes to the fore in the four special passages. This is why it is worth discussing them as a group. And since the term is now in common usage, I shall continue to call them Servant Songs.

Identifying the Servant

The four texts also have a number or common features that highlight their distinctiveness. These include the Lord's announcement of the servant (SS 1, 2, 4), his double role in relation to both Israel and the nations (SS 1, 2) and his suffering at the hands of others (SS 2, 3, 4). It is not any particular language or motif that sets these texts aside, but several interlinked features and themes.

We do not need to choose between isolating these texts and integrating them with their immediate context. There are both overlaps and distinctives

If we retain the Servant Songs, do they refer to the same entity? One extreme view is that of John Watts, who finds Cyrus in SS1, Israel and Cyrus or Darius in SS2, an anonymous leader in Jerusalem in SS3, and Zerubbabel in SS4.[10] But it is hard to believe that the author would have such different figures in mind and not provide clearer guidance for their identification. Peter Wilcox and David Paton-Williams find personified Israel in SS1–2, and Second Isaiah in SS3–4.[11] Joseph Blenkinsopp suggests that SS1 refers to Cyrus and SS2–4 refer to Second Isaiah, with SS4 written by a disciple after his death.[12]

An advantage of this last proposal is that it recognizes that several chapters separate Isaiah 42 from the others. This is significant because Second Isaiah has two parts. The first largely addresses Israel as a whole (Isaiah 40–48; introduced by Isa 40.1–8). The main problem is the exiles' physical location in Babylon and their political subjection to the Babylonian empire. But the Lord is about to raise up Cyrus to conquer Babylon (Isa 45.1–8), and this will solve both problems at once. Cyrus' victory will open up the way for the people to return. Israel can be certain that this will happen because the Lord is the incomparable God of creation (Isa 40.12–31) and history (Isaiah 41). The author mocks the gods of Babylon in biting satirical accounts of how idols are made (Isa 44.9–20). Isaiah 46.1–7 draws a dramatic contrast between the living God of Israel and the powerless gods of Babylon. The dominant emphasis (with the possible exception of SS1) is on the entire nation, which is called God's servant (Isa 41.8; 44.1; 45.4). As such Israel's task was to witness to the nations about the Lord's power and might (Isa 43.10, 12). The mood is confident and hopeful. The section ends with the stirring call, 'Go out from Babylon, flee from Chaldea' (Isa 48.20).

Israel can be certain because the Lord is the incomparable God of creation and history

Changing Focus

In the second part (Isaiah 49–55; anticipated by 40.9–11) a number of these themes disappear (Cyrus, Babylon, idols, the gods) and the focus turns to the restoration of Zion/Jerusalem. The major problem is now not external but internal: Israel's fearfulness and lack of faith. In the first part the prophet's fiery rhetoric assures the people of God's good purposes for them, and is aimed to overcome their reluctance (Isa 40.27; 43.1). The second part appears to recognize that this appeal did not meet with grateful acceptance and a packing of bags. This should not have been unexpected. The history of Israel made it abundantly clear that a far greater barrier to the nation's flourishing than any political or military threat was the people's sinfulness and disobedience, as Isaiah 1–39 sets out so vividly.

The prophets traced the basic problem to Israel's defective character and will, which the Old Testament locates in the heart. Exile was a necessary judgement on Israel's perennial disobedience, but would even that make any difference? The solution had to be more radical and get to the heart of the matter. The great exilic prophets recognized this problem and the need for a dramatic new way (Jer 17.9–10; Ezek 18.31). For Jeremiah this meant that there had to be a new covenant, in which the Lord wrote the law on the hearts of the Israelites (Jer 31.31–34). Ezekiel essentially makes the same point. He looked to a fundamental cleansing and renewal, through God's gift of a new spirit and a heart of flesh in place of a heart of stone (Ezek 36.25–28).

The Radical Solution

In Isaiah 49–55 the work of the second servant is the radical solution. The first Servant Song summoned the servant to be a light to the nations (Isa 42.6). This may well be a corporate reference, whether the nation or a group within the nation, in line with the other references to Israel/Jacob as servant. But in the second Song the servant is to bring Jacob/Israel back to the Lord, and takes on Israel's role amongst the nations (Isa 49.5-6). He also needs to restore the survivors of Israel, and this becomes the main theme of the third and fourth songs (Isa 49.6). The fourth Servant Song will explore with unparalleled depth how this might happen. Although there are still outbursts of praise in Isaiah 49–55, the presence of the last three songs modify the mood and make it more reflective. The final chapter perhaps acknowledges this with its emphasis on the certainty of God's word achieving his purposes, rather than Israel's response (Isa 55.10–11).

Who is the servant of Isaiah 53 and the other Songs?

We return to the most baffling question of all: who is the servant of Isaiah 53 and the other Songs? Readers of every generation have shared the Ethiopian eunuch's puzzlement: 'About whom, may I ask you, does the prophet say this?' (Acts 8.34). It is not clear whether the Songs are referring to a past, present or future figure. Some have thought it needs to be a figure from the past because this is indicated by the verbs. However, prophetic oracles often take the form of a visionary report of what will happen in the future as if it had already taken place (1 Kgs 22.17). The form of the verbs cannot by itself indicate the relation of the prophecy to its historical setting. The field of candidates is therefore wide open, and dozens of proposals have been made, none of them winning universal assent. It will be helpful to have a look at the main proposals. As I have already hinted, locating the servant's definite identity may not be the best approach, but a review will help clarify why this might be the case.[13]

The Servant as King

There is a great deal of royal language in the Songs, especially in SS1. The king is often called servant (1 Kgs 8.66; Ps 78.70) and is chosen (1 Sam 10.24; Ps 78.70; Isa 42.1). Earlier in Isaiah one of the great royal prophecies portrayed the king as being filled with the spirit (Isa 11.2; 42.1). Israel's hope was that their king would be exalted among the nations and that other kings would bow to him (Psalm 2; Isa 52.15). This would not just enhance his own wealth and prestige, but also witness to the power and glory of the Lord. It is also significant that a primary calling of the king is to establish justice (Ps 72.1–4; Isa 42.4).

The close relation between the servant and Israel also makes sense, because the king is the supreme representative of the people (2 Sam 19.43). In the history of scholarship several potential Israelite kings have been proposed: Uzziah, Hezekiah, Josiah, Jehoiachin, Sheshbazzar, Zerubbabel, Meshullam. But it might not be an Israelite king. Several contemporary scholars see the servant of SS1 as the Persian king Cyrus. It was he who opened up the way for them to return (2 Chron 36.22–23), and is even called the Messiah (the anointed one) by Second Isaiah (Isa 45.1). A common traditional view is that the servant is the Messiah. This is found in the early Aramaic paraphrase of the Old Testament, Targum Jonathan.

Can we identify the servant as the Messiah?

Yet, there are aspects of the servant's role that are rarely, if ever, associated with the king. Prominent among these is the teaching role (Isa 50.4). Unlike Jeremiah (Jer 23.5; 33) and Ezekiel (Ezek 34.23–24; 37.24–25), Second Isaiah marginalizes the Davidic hope. The only mention of David seems to set the royal line aside in favour of the people (Isa 55.3). In the later development of the messianic hope his royal character as a king of David's line is prominent. So this raises questions about whether we can identify the servant as the Messiah in any straightforward way.

The Servant as Prophet

The prophets are often called the Lord's servants (1 Kgs 14.18; Jer 7.25), and are called to their office (Isa 49.1; Jer 1.5). They are associated with teaching (Isa 8.16; 30.8–11), and are often rejected and suffer. The suffering endured by Jeremiah (*eg* Jer 11.19) and Ezekiel (*eg* Ezek 4.4-6) meant that some have proposed them as the servant. Perhaps the most popular option today is that the servant is Second Isaiah himself. This is the first proposal of the puzzled Ethiopian Eunuch as he shares his bafflement with Philip (Acts 8.34).

The main argument for this view is that the servant in SS2 and SS3 speaks in the first person, and the simplest reading of Isaiah 53 is that it is describing someone known to the readers. However, neither of these assumptions are necessarily true, and our ignorance of the person we call Second Isaiah means that any such proposal is a stab in the dark.[14] If his life and influence were as significant as is portrayed especially by Isaiah 53, it seems strange that we only know of him from these texts. Other objections are that prophets are not called to enact justice (Isa 42.1) and do not have an exalted future (Isa 52.13). Their role is to stand over against the people in communicating a word of judgement or salvation, not to act as their representative (Isa 49.3). While prophets can utter oracles against the nations, they are not called to convert them. Jonah is the exception that proves the rule.

The Servant as Israel

The strongest evidence for this is that Israel is frequently called God's servant in Isaiah 40–55 (Isa 41.8; 43.10). Israel is the one whom God upholds (Isa 41.10; 42.1) and is chosen by God (Isa 41.9; 42.1).[15] The servant is even explicitly called Israel in Isa 49.3, although in this same text the servant also has a mission to Israel (v 6). A corporate interpretation of the servant can still be retained if the reference is to a select group within Israel, similar to the remnant spoken of earlier in the book (Isa 10.20–22). It is natural for us in the West to think that the 'I' of the songs is an individual, but we belong in a highly individualistic culture. The Old Testament has plenty of examples where Israel is portrayed as an individual (*eg* Isa 1.5-6). For example, one interpretation of Psalm 23 is that the 'I' is Israel, not David or an individual. The great medieval Jewish exegetes generally saw in Isaiah 53 the sufferings of the Jewish people.[16]

But who might this select righteous group be? The prophets criticized every subsection of Israel, as well as the people as a whole. Prophets, priests, scribes, kings have all sinned, but the servant is righteous (Isa 50.5). The servant of the Songs also has an active mission, whereas Israel is primarily called to trust the Lord and believe in his word. The nature and extent of any proposed Israel within Israel is therefore unstable and ambiguous. A suggestion that goes some way to acknowledging this is that the Servant Songs demonstrate a progression from a more corporate figure in SS1 to a definite individual in SS4. This is a fitting progression in the light of the developing vision of what the servant is being called upon to do. The higher and the more demanding the task, the more difficult it is to imagine what kind of group would take up the role. Of course, this is also true as we try and imagine how a suitable individual could be found.

The Servant as Second Moses

Perhaps we should look back to the towering figure of Israel's beginning, Moses. There is a great deal of Exodus imagery in Isaiah 40–55. The return from exile will be like the journey through the wilderness that the Israelites had to undergo to reach the land (Isa 40.3–5). Indeed, part of the comfort and encouragement is that it will far surpass the first Exodus.

The Lord will provide water for them (Isa 41.17–18), but it will not be mere streams or pools, but rivers (Isa 43.19–20). He will accompany them when they pass through the waters (Isa 43.2), just as he did when the Israelites crossed the river Jordan (Joshua 3). The triumphant crossing over the Red Sea and the forces of chaos will be repeated as the Israelites return to Zion (Isa 51.9–11). The Israelites will be redeemed (Isa 41.14; 49.7), a key metaphor for the Exodus (Exod 15.13). So it makes sense for the person who leads Israel back to be another Moses, a second Moses.[17] He is not Moses reborn, but someone who inherits all of his gifts and authority. Like Moses, this new leader is called (Exod 3.4; 19.3) and frequently referred to as God's servant (Exod 14.31; Isa 63.11). Moses even sought to atone for his people (Exod 32.30–32). However, God does not accept Moses' offer to atone, and he is more a lawgiver than the one who establishes justice. Nor is he associated with wealth and exaltation.

The Servant as Zion/Jerusalem

Israel/Jacob is the main way in which the exiles are referred to in Isaiah 40–48. In the second part, where three of the four Servant Songs are to be found, the dominant figure for the people is as Zion/Jerusalem. The prominent role of Zion is anticipated in the stirring opening of Isaiah 40, where Zion is called to proclaim good news to the cities of Judah (Isa 40.9). Is the servant then perhaps the personified city of God? While Zion is mainly described as a woman, this is not the only image, and the masculine gender is sometimes used in the Hebrew verbs applied to the city (Isa 51.12, 14–16; *cf* Lam 3.1). Might the story of the servant be the story of the destruction and the restoration of the city?

The depth and intensity of the city's suffering is portrayed powerfully in the Book of Lamentations. However, this proposal meets the same challenge as that of other corporate identifications. The story of Zion and the story of the servant are indeed complementary in intriguing ways, making use of feminine and masculine ideals and hopes respectively.[18] But the extent of the bodily language of the Songs, especially in Isaiah 53, makes it difficult to see this as describing the hardships of the city. And there is little evidence of a righteous Zion within Zion. Rather, reading Isaiah 53 in context, the result of the work of the servant in restoring the people is that Zion is able to rejoice and enlarge her tent (Isa 54.1–3).

Choosing One Option

We could look at other options, but there are serious problems with each of them, and there is no scholarly consensus. Proving one option is impossible because of the extent to which the Songs are open and ambiguous. 'Servant' was a title used for numerous figures (including all of the above proposals), but we are given no clear hints that would enable us to narrow the field. There are words that have a more limited association with king, prophet, nation, but they effectively cancel each other out. We might take one or two of these into account by arguing for an expanded role, for example in proposing a teaching role for the king, a prophet acting as a second Moses. But we can only do this to a certain extent before we weaken severely our initial assumption about the servant's distinct identity.

4 A Better Way

The impossibility of identifying the servant has been an intense frustration for traditional historical criticism. David Clines has pointed out that historical critics have treated the text as 'a puzzle to be solved, a code to be cracked.'[19] But the inability of interpreters over the millennia to agree on an answer implies that they may be asking the wrong kind of question.

Worlds Behind, Within and In Front of the Text

Historical criticism has had as its main concern *the world behind the text*. It seeks to peer behind the present, later form of the text, and detect its underlying sources, and place them in their proper chronological context. It was natural for this school to seek the historical character behind the mysterious figure of the servant. But this search has failed. The servant comes to us as one unknown from a historical point of view.

Acknowledging this, Clines proposes that we focus on *the world of the text*, without worrying about its authorship or reference. He emphasizes the central role of unidentified pronouns (I, he, we, they) in Isaiah 53. Each of these has a particular character, and is related to the others in intriguing ways. Because these grammatical entities are undefined, the text becomes open to the reader's specific situation. We readers are invited to engage in a language event that can change our perception of our situation as we identify with one or other of the figures in the text. For example, someone who identifies with the figure who suffers in silence can become aware that this may be the will of the Lord. They can trust that their adoption of the role can have a powerful redemptive effect on the lives of others. The limitation of this approach is that it divorces the poem from any specific historical context, as well as its context in Second Isaiah and in the rest of Scripture. It is another short cut, albeit a sophisticated one. We leap from the past to the present in a powerful way, but without any reference to the long story of the people of God that provided the living context in which this text was read and applied.

There is, however, a third area of interpretive interest: *the world in front of the text*. An author, and especially a prophet, does not write in a cool, neutral and objective mood. On the contrary, their words are meant to be a fire that consumes careless sinners, and a hammer that breaks the rocklike immobility and apathy of hearers (Jer 23.29). A prophetic oracle, like a sermon, is meant not so much to inform as to transform. The intention is to bring hearers face to face with the living God and for them to hear the Torah, his Lord's teaching and instruction for their lives. The prophets employ their utmost rhetorical efforts in order to overcome the deaf ears and the blind eyes of the people. The purpose of the text is rooted in the exilic context, but continues to speak to future generations, whose lives reflect the same failings and hopes expressed in Isaiah 40–55.

The Kind of Servant God Needs

But what is that purpose? John Goldingay has memorably proposed that they are a job description. They set out the character and role of the kind of servant that God needs.[20] The ambiguity and openness of the text arise because of a recognition that something brand new was needed, but that who or what this might be was as yet unknown. The story of Israel has shown with abundant clarity that none of the previous servants had succeeded in enabling Israel to become the people it was supposed to be. The kings were meant to rule with humility and wisdom, but they had looked to their own interests and worshipped other gods. Even the best of them (a Hezekiah or a Josiah) failed to make a significant impact on the people.

As for the prophets, they were indeed passionate and obedient, but their message was met with disdain and mockery. Their effectiveness was marginal and the people preferred to listen to the false prophets who proclaimed peace and plenty. There were classes of people who were meant to serve in an exemplary way, but they were all compromised and had little impact on the nation for the good. So, this approach suggests, the prophet attempts something new: a job description that combines aspects of king, prophet and godly remnant. In faith and hope the author of the Servant Songs sets out a job description for the ideal servant, and trusts that God will raise up a suitable applicant, or applicants.

The author of the Servant Songs sets out a job description for the ideal servant

Jim Adams explores how Second Isaiah, and particularly the Servant Songs, are self-involving texts. They are not neutral descriptions, but invite readers to make the text their own and treat it as a dramatic script for their lives.[21] The use of the same term, servant, for both Israel and the one described in the text encourages this identification. But it is also possible to identify with the sinful 'we,' who did not recognize the servant, but now wonder at the amazing benefits that came from his death. The difficulty is that the gulf between these roles is huge. How is it possible to move from the 'we' to the 'he'? We are back to the problem of who could or would dare to take on the servant's role.

For this job description looks like those setting out such a list of requirements that even the archangel Gabriel would be shown the door. Who could possibly satisfy all the required qualities, skills and experiences set out in the Servant Songs? One possible response is that what is impossible from a human perspective is possible for God (Mark 10.27). Moreover, this impossibility is present in the Scriptures from the very beginning. It is the baffling mystery why God continued the story after the sin of Adam and Eve, the story of Israel after the golden calf incident, the story of the monarchy after the Bathsheba affair. How can his promises and purposes be fulfilled, given the reality of human pride and deep-set sinfulness? How can God promise to save a people whose disobedience and rebellion are seen in every chapter of the story?

Finding a Suitable Candidate

The lack of suitable candidates continues to be evident in the centuries that followed the writing of Isaiah 53. There were no great figures that could be seen as fulfilling even a portion of the servant's role. Elements of the prophecies are recycled as Israel's hope for the future was developed and expanded. There are probably references to Isaiah 53 in several obscure passages in the Book of Zechariah. There is the striking of a shepherd and scattered sheep (Zech 13.7; Isa 53.4). Zechariah also portrays a suffering figure ('whom they have pierced,' Zech 12.10), although the word used is not found in Second Isaiah. Zechariah brings the identity of this figure into line with the rest of the prophets in relating him to the house of David (Zech 12.7–13.1). Redemption is there too, though using different language. The result of this figure's suffering will be the purification of the inhabitants of Jerusalem from sin and impurity (Zech 13.1).

For Christians the promises and prophecies of the Old Testament comprise a mystery that is only resolved by a matching mystery: the man of Nazareth. Who is this person who did not conform to any of the standard categories: a king, but a hidden one; a prophet, but more than a prophet; the holy one of God, but not a priest? Later it becomes clear that in Jesus Christ God himself has entered the fray and declared the candidacy of his Son for the impossible role of servant of the Lord. For as Second Isaiah affirms with utmost clarity, only God can save. Only a Jesus who is both fully human and fully divine can resolve the mystery at the heart of the Old Testament. Only he can bear our sins and make many righteous.

Only a Jesus who is both fully human and fully divine can resolve the mystery

The Definitive Performance

If the Servant Songs are a job description, then Jesus takes up their immense challenge and gives them a supreme and definitive performance. As the servant he is a representative of Israel. This typology lies behind a number of his actions, such as his wanderings in the desert for forty days and being tempted, as Israel was on the way from Sinai to the promised land. His responses to the devil in the words of Deuteronomy are paradigms of how Israel was meant to behave, but did not (Matt 4.1–11; Luke 4.1–13). But this is no simple fulfilment. The move from forty years to forty days demonstrates how Jesus interprets the Scriptures flexibly and realistically.

This demonstrates how Jesus interprets the Scriptures flexibly and realistically

His compassionate ministry sums up the ideal of Isa 42.3 ('a bruised reed he will not break, and a dimly burning wick he will not quench'), while Isa 50.2 articulates his ministry of teaching and encouragement ('The Lord GOD has given me the tongue of a teacher, that I may know how to sustain the weary with a word'). The Passion narratives work out the notes of opposition and suffering that become more and more evident in the Servant Songs (Isa 49.4; 50.6) until they come to a climax in Isaiah 53. The detailed story told in the gospels could not be predicted from the Servant Songs, but the overall theme of Jesus' suffering on behalf of others is evident in hindsight. The vindication of the suffering servant is amply demonstrated in the resurrection and ascension of Jesus. The fulfilment goes well beyond the starting text in unexpected and surprising ways. The vertical imagery of vindication ('lifted up') is clear, but would normally be understood metaphorically (Isa 52.13). The spatial dimension is given an entirely new dimension of meaning in Luke's account of Jesus' ascension and translation to heaven (Acts 1.9–10).

The Servant and the Nations

What about the servant's role towards the nations? It is here that Jesus perhaps provides the most surprising and radical interpretation of the Songs. From very early on he saw his role as happening in two stages. In his earthly ministry he was clear that he was only sent to the lost sheep of the house of Israel (Matt 15.24). His first job was to renew and remake the people of God around himself. The end of this initial stage was in Jerusalem, not the ends of the earth. Yet Jesus, in alignment with the prophets and particularly the Servant Songs, is also clear that the God of Israel is to reign over all the nations. His servant role will enable this to happen, but not directly (Isa 49.4; 49.6; 52.15).

Again, it is a realistic awareness that one person cannot do everything. Rather, this will happen through the redeemed people of God, now centred around

Jesus and empowered by the Spirit (Matt 29.18–20; Mark 4.30–32; Luke 24.47–49). Since justice has not been established among the nations, the job of the servant is not finished, but continues in the servant calling of the church. There are unique aspects to the work of Christ, but it is Christians who are called to extend his ministry to the ends of the earth.

Interpreting Isaiah 53

5

In this chapter I shall try and apply some of these insights to the greatest of the Servant Songs, Isaiah 53. It is easy to get caught up in the detail, especially since the Hebrew is often difficult to understand. Instead I shall look at four prominent themes that recur and can be the basis for a broader reflection: the servant's suffering, innocence, atoning work and exaltation.

Suffering

The range and intensity of the images and metaphors for suffering is remarkable. From a physical point of view he is struck down, afflicted, wounded, crushed and bruised. The suffering of the servant culminates in death, when he is cut off from the land of the living and makes his grave with the wicked. Social stigma matches the physical suffering. Being regarded with honour and respect is central to identity and well-being in traditional cultures. But the appearance of the servant is marred, perhaps activating the motif that evil is evident in the face. He is despised and rejected, and people hide their faces from him.

The dishonour continues in death, since his life and character are now permanently associated with those with whom he is buried, the rich and the wicked. The verb 'struck down' is particularly evocative, for it is often associated with the 'leper' of Leviticus 13–14 (this was probably some kind of skin disease). This terrible disease was not so much a physical as a social horror, since its high level of impurity required the separation and isolation of the sufferer, and made normal life impossible.

Some interpreters do not find in this passage a physical death, merely a degree of suffering that brings the servant to the very borders of death. We can compare how the exiles picture themselves as dead bones (Ezek 37.11), and Jonah portrays himself in the land of the dead (Jonah 2.6). As for the grave, it is not yet occupied, but merely assigned to him (the verb is open to this interpretation, as in Ezek 39.11).[22] However, a real death seems to make the best sense of the story being told. The dark climax of death is required to do justice to its polar opposite, the exaltation of the servant. The poem portrays life and death in its fullest sense. While the narrative tells of a real death, it is possible that the poet intended it to be applied metaphorically to any real candidate. The idea of individual resurrection from the dead is a very late entry into the social imagination of the Old Testament (clear only in Dan 12.1–3). Again, we can see in Jesus the unexpected but fitting turning of metaphor into history.

Innocence

A second key theme is the servant's innocence. This sets up the central tension of the poem in that the servant's suffering is completely undeserved. This is prominent in the latter part of the poem. The servant did not open his mouth, despite the fact that his suffering was due to a perversion of justice (vv 7–8). He was innocent both in word ('there was no deceit in his mouth,' v 9) and in deed ('he had done no violence,' v 9). He is called the righteous one (v 11). He is the servant in whom the Lord, unlike those around him, finds no fault.

Atonement

The resolution of this tension is the third motif: the redemptive power of undeserved suffering. Its location at the centre of the poem emphasizes its importance. Again, the images used for both problem and solution are multiple and only the overall movement of the story unifies them. The 'he' of the servant takes the place of the 'we' who are looking on.[23] Isaiah 53 highlights the metaphor of sin as disease. Both of these affect our whole being and have potentially deadly consequences. The curses of the covenant (Lev 26.14–39; Deut 28.15–57) emphasize the physical consequences of sin, which are reflected in the physical suffering of the servant, who takes on the guilt of the 'we.' Thus the servant bears our sicknesses and carries our pains (Isa 53.4), so that we are healed by his bruises (v 5).

Isaiah 53 highlights the metaphor of sin as disease

Sin is also rebellion against God. The two words for sin and rebellion in v 5 recall the opening accusation at the very beginning of Isaiah (Isa 1.2, 4). They highlight the perennial failing of Israel to be the obedient covenant people that they were meant to be. But the consequences of these failings are now taken vicariously by the servant. The same point is made through the standard metaphor of the Lord as shepherd and Israel as his flock. The metaphor is adapted to the context. These sheep stray not by accident or stupidity, but because they have deliberately gone their own way, and the servant has carried their iniquity and been slaughtered on their behalf (Isa 53.6–7).

Exaltation

The fourth and final motif is the exaltation of the servant. This is the unexpected reversal that changes the story from tragedy to glory. From the depths of the grave (Isa 53.9) the servant is exalted, lifted up and made very high (Isa 52.13). There is a profound contrast between those seeking to exalt themselves (Isa 2.12–14), and those whom the Lord raises up to his own high and lofty status (Isa 6.1; 33.10; 57.15). The poem is set at a time when those who observed the servant's suffering now recognize his achievements. But his vindication will transcend any national boundaries, as kings and nations marvel at him (Isa 52.15).

Applying Isaiah 53

These four motifs are open to multiple applications. We can look to the past to see those who have contributed to the job description, albeit in a limited and imperfect way. We can see anticipations especially in the foundational figures of Abraham, Moses and David. All three find hardship and suffering as they seek to follow the Lord. They are (relatively) innocent of charges brought against them, and choose the path of humility and even potential death. Thus Abraham gives up Isaac (Genesis 22), Moses risks death in confronting Pharaoh (Exod 2.15), and David allows Saul to live despite the threat to his life (1 Samuel 24). These acts of obedience lead to positive consequences, even if this is not as explicit as the redemptive suffering portrayed in Isaiah 53. The covenant promises are renewed for Abraham (Gen 22.15–18), Moses successfully intercedes for Israel (Ps 106.23), and David receives the kingship and an everlasting covenant (2 Sam 23.5). All of them are now regarded as heroes of the faith, even though their flaws are evident and compromise their story in a way that is not true of the servant of Isaiah 53.

We do not know whether Second Isaiah, or someone like him, was another exemplar who influenced the portrayal in Isaiah 53, as various scholars have speculated. But we do know from the gospels how Jesus gave the supreme performance of the text. It is not that every detail of the text is fulfilled. Rather, like a virtuoso jazz performer, Jesus adds new elements that are consistent with it, but go far beyond what might be imagined. The gospel writers in turn select and highlight further features as they retell the story. Thus the gospels demonstrate in numerous ways how Jesus is innocent of the charges laid against him. His opponents can find no fault in his behaviour, and in his trial false witnesses accuse him. His uniqueness in this and other respects ultimately brings about the acknowledgement of his divine nature. Crucifixion was well enough known that the gospels saw no need to dwell on the intensity of Jesus' sufferings. As in Isaiah 53 the suffering was social as well as physical. Jesus is crucified naked in the sight of women as well as men. But it is at the cross that we find the first recognition of the power of this innocent suffering, as the penitent thief asks Jesus to remember him (Luke 23.39–43). The rest of the New Testament is then a series of further variations as it explores assorted metaphors that further elucidate how Christ died for our sin and thereby wrought forgiveness.

But the servant role is not exhausted by the work of Christ. Peter applies the example of Christ to his hearers when he cites Isaiah 53 (1 Pet 2.21–25). Although here it is a matter of gaining God's approval, other New Testament texts suggest something more. In a remarkable text Paul states that 'I am now rejoicing in my sufferings for your sake, and in my flesh I am completing what is lacking in Christ's afflictions for the sake of his body, that is, the church (Col 1.24).' The same interchange we find in Isaiah 53 and Paul sees the redeeming power of Christ's death continued in his own sufferings.

We tend to think that sin, guilt and punishment are a matter for individuals, but the New Testament works with familial metaphors that understand life in more corporate categories. A mother or father can represent the family on behalf of the failures or the triumphs of their children. The flourishing or withering of the church almost always depends on the selfless service of various individuals who seek to follow Jesus Christ. Their commitment and often unrecognized sacrifice bear fruit in the lives of those who do not appreciate what they are doing, at least for some time. But eventually, and perhaps only when the book of life is opened, their deeds will be made known and they shall receive their reward as servants of God (Rev 11.18; 20.12).

Is Jesus the Answer?

So is Isaiah 53 a prophecy about Jesus or not? It is possible to answer both yes and no. From a historical perspective, the openness of the text allows Christians to read it as an anticipation of Jesus' astonishing fulfilment of the hopes crystalized in this portrait of a servant. But this depends on a larger and broader interpretation of the Scriptures as telling a story that comes to a climax in Christ (Luke 24.27). But while Christians are convinced of the truth of the New Testament account, they need to acknowledge with humility that others come to different conclusions. As happens in the Book of Acts, there is call for honest conversation and debate.

But the Servant Songs are far more than part of a Christological puzzle. For we are not mere observers, but readers who are invited to move from a neutral stance to an active identification with the 'we,' and then the 'he.' As God's unique servant Jesus came to bear our guilt and punishment, but this did not exhaust the universal vision of the Servant Songs. Jesus himself recognized this when he passed on to his disciples the job of proclaiming the good news to the ends of the earth (Matt 28.18–20). From this perspective Isaiah 53 is a text that invites all who read it to take up the job of a servant. They are to continue Christ's work of bringing light and forgiveness to the nations, whatever it costs.

Notes

1 For example Grünewald's *Crucifixion*. See https://www.wikiart.org/en/matthias-grunewald/the-isenheim-altarpiece-1516

2 https://www.sefaria.org/Isaiah.53.3?lang=bi&with=Rashi&lang2=en For a survey of Jewish interpretation see Marc Brettler and Amy-Jill Levine, 'Isaiah's Suffering Servant: Before and after Christianity,' *Interpretation,* 73 (2019), 158–173.

3 For helpful perspective on these issues, see Richard S Briggs, *Reading Isaiah: A Beginner's Guide* (Grove Biblical booklet B55).

4 For a review of the scholarly debate about the composition of Isaiah see H G M Williamson, *The Book Called Isaiah: Deutero-Isaiah's Role in Composition and Redaction* (Oxford: Clarendon Press, 1994).

5 See the classic treatment in F F Bruce, *This Is That: The New Testament Development of Some Old Testament Themes* (Exeter: Paternoster, 1968).

6 The classic study is Gordon J Wenham, *'Betûlāh* 'a Girl of Marriageable Age',' *Vetus Testamentum,* 22/3 (1972), 326–348.

7 Hugh G M Williamson, *Variations on a Theme: King, Messiah and Servant in the Book of Isaiah* (Carlisle: Paternoster Press, 1998).

8 Bernhard Duhm, *Das Buch Jesaia* (Göttingen: Vandenhoeck and Ruprecht, 1892) pp 277–278.

9 Tryggve N D Mettinger, *A Farewell to the Servant Songs: A Critical Examination of an Exegetical Axiom* (Lund: CWK Gleerup, 1983).

10 John D W Watts, *Isaiah 34–66* (Waco, TX: Word Publishing, rev edn, 2006).

11 Peter Wilcox and David Paton-Williams, 'The Servant Songs in Deutero-Isaiah,' *JSOT,* 42 (1988), 79–102.

12 Joseph Blenkinsopp, *Isaiah 40–55: A New Translation with Introduction and Commentary* (New York: Doubleday, Anchor Bible 19a, 2002) pp 76–79.

13 The standard survey is Christopher R North, *The Suffering Servant in Deutero-Isaiah: An Historical and Critical Study* (Oxford University Press, 1948). This includes most of the options discussed by later authors.

14 Some scholars find several authors or traditions in Isaiah 40–55, so that the identity of Second Isaiah become even vaguer. However, a succession of editors is rarely responsible for the creation of a work of exceptional literary artistry.

15 This is an early interpretation of the Septuagint, which translates 'Israel my chosen' in Isa 42.1.

16 North, *Suffering Servant, op cit,* pp 17–20.

17 G P Hugenberger, 'The Servant of the Lord in the "Servant Songs" of Isaiah: A Second Moses Figure,' in Philip E Satterthwaite, Richard S Hess and Gordon J Wenham (eds), *The Lord's Anointed: Interpretation of Old Testament Messianic Texts* (Carlisle: Paternoster, 1995).

18 John F A Sawyer, 'Daughter of Zion and Servant of the Lord in Isaiah: A Comparison,' *Journal for the Study of the Old Testament,* 44 (1989), 89–107.

19 D J A Clines, *I, He, We and They* (Sheffield: JSOT Press, 1976).

20 John Goldingay, *God's Prophet, God's Servant: A Study in Jeremiah and Isaiah 40–55* (Carlisle: Paternoster Press, 1994) p 92.

21 Jim W Adams, *The Performative Nature and Function of Isaiah 40–55* (New York: T and T Clark, 2006).

22 For such a reading see the Jewish commentator Shalom M Paul, *Isaiah 40-66: Translation and Commentary* (Grand Rapids, MI: Eerdmans, 2012) pp 406–409.

23 Bernd Janowski, 'He Bore Our Sins: Isaiah 53 and the Drama of Taking Another's Place,' in Peter Stuhlmacher (ed), *The Suffering Servant: Isaiah 53 in Jewish and Christian Sources* (Grand Rapids, MI: Eerdmans, 2004) pp 48–74. This is perhaps the clearest biblical articulation of a theme that will become central in the New Testament and later theology.